I See Them Now

I See Them Now

Poems by Alissa Sammarco
Photographs by Alissa Sammarco

Turning Point

Published by Turning Point
P.O. Box 541106
Cincinnati, OH 45254-1106

ISBN: 9781625494535

Poetry Editor: Kevin Walzer
Business Editor: Lori Jareo

Visit us on the web at www.turningpointbooks.com

Cover Art: Susan Crew
Author Photo: Troi Gray

This book is dedicated to David, Elliott and Peter,
who will always be my babies.

Thanks to Robert for the love and support, the never ending.

Thanks to Sheila Na Gig and Black Moon Magazine for publishing
There are Some Words I Just Can't Bring With Me,
and to Change Seven for publishing *Snapshots #1 and #2.*

Contents

I will be old one day
crow's feet in the corner of my mind,
but not today, I say,
not today.

I See Them Now

In that place
between boy and man,
and like spring trees,
just a hint
upon the chin,
a dusting of green
along the branch
until suddenly,
sprout full leaves
and cotton tree seeds
that fly away
on the wind.

When Boys and Girls Dream of One Another

I remember all those years ago
when I was happy and you were too.
We spent our summers giggling,
flirting with the camp counselor,
all of us named the same.
Alice, Lisa, Elise.

We spent our days in bathing suits,
pulling lake grass from our toes,
squealing when it brushed our bellies as we swam,
laying on docks in sun kissed bodies.
Alice, Lisa, Elise.

We ran everywhere, too excited to walk,
too impatient to wait one second more
to meet up at the rock. Just a rock.
Its memorial plaque long unread.

We made noise until old ladies shushed us from windows,
floral nightgowns waiving us home.
We scattered into the lamplight,
boys and girls dreaming of one another.

Russian Palaces

I visited my summer place,
walking through the painted ladies,
their porches bound tight
to protect them from winter
that transforms them into Russian palaces,
buried in antiquity under drifts of snow.
I remember boys who pulled my braids
and girls giggling, our heads together.
Some lost forever to our Father above,
others lost to their own demons,
and those who return to this place
to raise their children,
here, where time is wrapped
in canvas shrouds like these houses.

Where Childhood Lives

I can still find that place where childhood lives.
Each night I ran with you
under the milky way, the moon, the stars,
out on the field where we played ball by day,
the fresh cut grass stinging our noses
and we lay face toward the sky,
holding hands and giggling,
telling secrets to each other
about boys, too young to be lovers.

At the witching hour
between two and three
we were free.

But now the years smell sour
like an old woman's breath,
and although our secrets are still kept,
we do not share them,
even when we visit that place
where we lived so long ago.

In My Mother's Bedroom

Her jewelry box lay on a lace doily
with the shell comb and brush,
and her pearls from last night.

It seemed like hours, examining each piece,
slipping rings on fingers,
a bracelet of silver geese
in an endless circle, tail to beak.

A string of pearls hung on my neck,
they swung back and forth
as I shifted my feet,
at any second, fearing her step.

Her box was lined with velvet secrets.
While mine had shells from Holden Beach,
whispering in my ear,
secrets of seas not yet sailed.

And counting the days since she left me,
examining these geese, tail to beak,
listening for seashells' secrets they no longer speak,

I cannot recall whether they were ever mine to keep.

I Have Become My Mother

Entombing memories where they can't hurt,
locking time in tiny drawers,
in boxes stacked in the back of the closet.

I keep a light on my key ring,
but I cannot find the lock.

I have become my mother losing my roar.
If I swallow the medicine,
will my voice return?

The day will come drifting in like mist
when pain and joy cast no shadows

even though the sun still rises and sets,
my heart beats the rhythm of regret
for children born and unborn.

Oh, faithless women,
where will we lay our head.

There are Some Words I Just Can't Bring with Me

I open my mouth and like spring waters,
they seep out, soaking the earth
until they find their course,
navigating the contours of rocks
and pockmarked game trails of suburban deer.
Gravity pulls them over and under tree roots,
carrying away the leaves that festered all winter.
Suddenly, the gunk and its smell,
matted, wet and moldy,
are gone. I've found the courage
to say what I mean.

My mother said that I have holes in my memory.
She would visit my house and leave clues for me,
a bible with her notes,
a book entitled "Finding A Way Out,"
a teacup with bourbon.
Clues to remember what filled those holes,
to save me from my gaslighter
when he turned the lights down a little more each day.
He hid in the basement until the slightest insult
sent him piercing through our floors
like a bullet through glass.

I am Pisces, a creature of water,
shape shifting to fill the buckets
he left out for me.
Until I spilled out, leaving puddles everywhere
for the boys to splash on rainy days.

She said I have holes in my memory.
Pieces broken off when they were too sharp.
I threw them in the stew-pot until they melted,
eating them for dinner so that
they couldn't poison us all.

Everything is Small Again

I think for me the end came
to girlhood, dressed in flowered shifts,
when everything big was small again.

That was when on tiptoes I no longer strained
to reach my cup and quench my thirst.
I think for me the end came

as quickly as the kick-the-can game
shrank from miles to steps
and everything big was small again.

I hardly felt like a grown-up the day
I traded my shifts for boxing mitts,
though I know for me the end came

as I went to war, my flaming mane
set fire to my opponents in competitions stiff.
The rites of passage, a woman made,
and everything big is small again.

Twilight

my picture posted on the internet
with hair and makeup
Cheshire smiles
stealing the last moments

of ageless beauty

before the fairy-tale light
washes across my face
leaving only shadows

Mirror Mirror

If you asked me to put words to it,
I couldn't. But each time
I catch a glimpse
reflected in the storefront window,
in the mirror as I leave the house,
I see you, a generation apart.
But the slant of the eye,
maybe the crook of a smile,
the way the hair curls out
instead of in. I don't have your
blue eyes, and the sadness,
that is mine. Your eyes
danced, sparkling like
sequins on a little girl's tutu.
Smiles shining like patent leather
and as fleeting as a shadow
slipped out of sight.

Family Arrives for The Feast

The season has turned.
Rosy cheeks puff plumes into the air.
They are dreams that rise, white and ethereal,
fading like sleep from our eyes
as the family arrives.

They come in from rain drenched streets,
the water squishing into their shoes
as they tiptoe across the lawn.
It is the morning of the feast.

Coffee greets them,
that elixir, hot and cloudy,
brewed from the belly of our beginnings
and shared bittersweet with honey and cream.

The children return, believing they are adults.
They moved away and learned
how to fold laundry and navigate groceries.
They will always be our babies.

We remember the rules we must follow,
maintaining civility with smiles and laughter,
singing refrains of our legacy,
the crazy aunt with her parade of ribbons and bells.
No one mentions she is naked.
Tales of adventure and undoing are told again and again.
But the chorus of bitterness
that echoes through the years,
keeps silent this day.

Finally, the moment has arrived.
There is a pause.
Then the ooh's and ah's as Pops approaches, scalpel in hand,
dissecting the bird, categorizing its contents.

We sit together and give thanks for this day,

before we devour it, the wine and water,
washing down all stubbornness between us.

Have We Forgotten

Have we forgotten who we are?
Warriors soaked in blood –
of both enemies and friends.

No war is won without loss
and the ground is steeped
in the blood of brothers,
fighting with sticks and rocks.

Our heritage built on foundation
of bricks baked with the bones of our foes.
It holds back the waters
keeping safe mothers and daughters.
We are not lost.

On Your 82nd Birthday

I am glad to sit with you,
just for a few minutes
even though the sun is very hot today
between bursts of thunderstorms
and rainbows.

I brought you yellow roses.
You always liked
sunflowers, their brown eyes
wide open to the world.

I'll just stay a few minutes
here where the grass feels soft
under my feet, waiting
for the rain to return.

I watch the white moths
that flutter on the bush nearby.
But they seem far away and fuzzy
like I am the memory
and they are looking at me.

I try to smell the greenness
of the grass, full summer leaves.
But I smell only the musty earth,
waiting for its inhabitant,
waiting for a tear to escape my eye,
like I was the one who left
and you are remembering me.

I hold my breath, reset my senses,
but my lungs burn
and I breach the surface, gasping.
You are still right here where I left you,
laughing and irreverent;
your eyes melting into the sky,
until I must walk away,
back to the day and night and day again.

I'll just stay a few minutes
and visit, even though
the sun is very hot today.

The Night Before We Buried You

I woke up at three a.m. as I often do.
It was a child's nightmare
that startled me.
The night before we buried you
that hour came in siren winds.
In a perfect storm of yesterdays and tomorrows,
I was Quan Yin,
my foot upon the serpent's head,
the sea crashing beneath my feet.
I thought I conquered the chaos
when suddenly, the tears erupted
like surf spit out through the hole in the cliff,
wetting my cheeks with ocean spray
as I remembered you.

Autumn

I woke to Autumn,
its bouquet of burnt umber and chartreuse
rocking in gusts off the ridge.

Driving down the highway,
I watch the sky
press against treetops
that hold the clouded canopy at bay.

It is with their last breath
they surrender to winter.

All That Jazz

We drove down to Schwartz's Point,
a turn of the century building
squeezed into the fifth corner
of Vine and McMicken.
Stone standard, tall and thin.
"Where do you go in?" I asked.

In the window the sign read
LIVE JAZZ.
Painted, not neon.
White on black, like the milky air inside
before they banned cigarettes,
before they banned us,
the music, the smoke,
a soup of yellowed teeth and tobacco-stained fingers
calloused from strings and pounding lungs
blowing that horn, sweet and steady.

I miss that jazz.
The closeness of the air,
the sweetness of the smell
of whiskey and perfume,
of men in white fedoras
and women in black cut dresses.

I miss that jazz.
Losing the feeling of time passing
as minutes turn to hours
with each clink of ice.
I promised myself, only Diet Pepsi

fizzy yet flat.
Until a man at the bar
sent over a proper glass,
and I tipped my smile his way
and worked no more that day
as amber over ice filled me
and the warm jazz transformed me
from ice into water,
liquid and divine.

The Heretic

Even your holy words
could not stop it from happening.
The breakup of everything,
the division of our faith,
our fellowship.

We are Human.
The lessons of Babel
teach that it is
inevitable.

We do not speak the same
language, yet sometimes,
for a short while, we pretend
to understand.

The tower always falls
scattered by our own
pride.

It is how
He made us,
struggling to overcome
our inescapable
inheritance.

Heaven
(After *Sanctuary* by Ada Limon)

Should I shout at you in my grandmother's voice?
She gave it to me when I was a girl,
wisking bits of hair from my forehead
and stirring pots of sauce over coals
in a kitchen full of electricity.

She gave it to me so I'd know what to say
when the men tracked their in mud at the end of the day.

Know what to say when aching arms and backs
scooped up little legs and shoulders,
tumbling them into the car for a drive to the beach.

Know what to say when sandwiches, salted with sand,
filled little bellies and hearts and hands
while the ocean blew summer away,
shouting at the top of her lungs.

Snapshot #1: Picture of Pots on The Deck

In the morning, before the sun gets hot and the mosquitoes arrive, I visit my garden, wandering through her buds and blooms, wondering what changes I will find – who has died and who has grown tall. Every morning, the sun touches my temples. This house is new to me. I struggle to call it my house, my home. I struggle to accept the gift of it, and the desire to make it mine, too. I moved in and each time we discuss a repair, or a project, each time we clean the garage or buy new sheets for the bed, he corrects me. "Our house." He says. "Our bed." He says. But he never says, "Our garden".

I spend hours staring at the pots. I pluck a geranium's yellowed leaf, and clip her exhausted booms, making room for the next one. I prick my thumb on the rose bush which causes my finger to get infected. I buy bags of potting soil, and reuse the plastic nursery pots, making new geranium plants and Wandering Jews with their purple hearts. I add Black Eyed Susan and Sun Flowers, happy and yellow. But the seeds I brought with me from my old house, the ones I saved and preserved to grow here, they do not sprout.

He pretends not to watch me while reading the paper and drinking coffee. He makes us breakfast, he even eats what I cook, and we share our meal amidst the jungle. He stays quiet while I talk about each new bud I've noticed, or how the Forget Me Nots are about to bloom. He knows it is what I need, that piece that I call my own, that corner of "our house".

Snapshot #2: Picture from the Norris Dam

We went on vacation to Tennessee, leaving our Ohio River Valley for those of Appalachia. I took a picture from on top of the dam. We could see across the valleys and from hilltop to hilltop. He held my hand as we walked on top. He does not like to walk across bridges. What is this great expanse I live in? Have I forgotten the flow and ebb of the rivers? Forgotten the oceans? Tides rise and fall, but have I forgotten the moon that pushes and pulls the tide inside of me.

There was a time when I could not see the expanse. I do not know if I was afraid of its greatness, or simply afraid to take my eyes off of the job, the kids, the Ex. Take my eyes off the floor so that I would not crush any eggshells as I traversed my own kitchen. Those days had ceilings. They had rooms with doors and curtains that closed. They had fear that someone would know I lived in the dark.

But everything changes. For me, it was when I walked out of the house my Ex and I built. I turned out the lights. I handed the keys over. On that day, I saw the clouds and they looked like the underside of the sandy ocean bottom. I saw them moving and shifting and changing moods.

On a day not unlike today, with the cloudbursts, and in between, rainbows, we looked out from the dam. We could see the next county, the next state. Tennessee changes color at each rolling peak. She is like a woman, soft and warm.

I cannot tell you that all is calm, or that the ceiling does not close in on me. However, here in the Ohio river valley, the river flows southwest, and the clouds fly northeast. In the space between, I feel the breeze and smell the lightning and taste the rain. It is there I feel the sun and shiver a little in the night when autumn comes. It is there, planting wildflower seeds across my lawn, that I can breathe.

Letter To My Bipolar Son

It wasn't like I didn't
know you were different. You
told me about visitors,
whispering to you, you went
where time bent sideways, spinning,
like looking in fun-house glass,
losing yourself in their lies.

A Boy at the Gallery

I would have found him
        if he hadn't found me
standing apart from everything
        in the gallery.
Surrounded by the suggestions
        of O'Keeffe with leaves of red,
or bright orange sunsets,
        harbinger of summer's end.
His bright clear voice,
        in the silence it seemed loud,
announcing his chicken-dog dance
        to the silent crowd
who stood in front of paintings,
        pale faced and proud.

"You know I made it up,"
        As he shot his arrow across the room.
"Yes," Watching it
        strike the target of red, yellow and blue.

The Unicorn and the Whale

What happy bedfellows,
the unicorn and the whale,
living one on the land
and the other in the sea.
Magic sprouted wings,
they took to the air,
a cyclone spin
lifting them high,
feathers bound
by wax and gum,

melting
                    melting

kissed by the sun.
Their hearts beating faster
until they could not
hold their breath.
Exhaling, at the wind's death
and falling,
like all lovers fall,
piece by piece
back to earth.

This is My Sad Book

Pages dimpled from tears
with jazz and gin,
ice rattling at two a.m.
I have another book where love
abounds. Hands finding hearts,
lips softly part. With rum
under paper umbrellas
hiding from the sun.
I have another book for melodies,
sweet tragic Aeschylus' autumn leaf.
From time to time, I can't recall,
which one is honest, which says it all,
around the hour of two a.m.
while ice rattles with jazz and gin.

She Speaks Like Water

She speaks like water,
words expanding rings across the surface
then racing out, tumbling rocks

with the trilling of her tongue.
Those gentle songs that were sung
when you lay together, under the willows.

She quenched your thirst
with her secret fire water
kept cold in the fold of her skirts.

She is demure yet unforgiving
as she cuts through granite,
clearing your path.

Unable to resist, you follow,
then turn away, disobedient.
Her voice grows loud,

rapid and angry, spilling out
in full throated frenzy
to the rocks below

until her roar becomes calm,
and once again, her song
lures you back to its medicine.

Formidable

The greatest man in my life
was not the one I loved best.
He was not kind, he was formidable.

The kind of person who tasks you,
and in the end, you know exactly who you are.

His words ring in my ears long after the day we parted.
And although I still know his face,
it does not haunt me or come unbidden at night.

Unlike the pounding in my breast
to be formidable.

Postcard to a Friend

Dear S,

I found this postcard behind the bookcase.
The tropical sunset is worn, its edges tattered, like the memory of us.
Can I still call you friend after such a long journey apart?

Forever, A.

Made in the USA
Columbia, SC
04 February 2024

31272899R00027